This book is dedicated to all families of medically complex children who wish for simple adventures for their children.

For days, weeks, and months,
I sat wondering at home

I dreamed of the faraway
lands I would roam.

Neyland, Omphalocele
Granger, Omphalocele
Everett, Trisomy 21 and CHD
Rosalyn, Oral Dysphasia
Elizabeth, Idiopathic
Pulmonary Hemorrhage

But I have some tubes and devices, you see...

And they keep me tethered when I want to break free.

Mia, Trisomy 18
Elsie, Trisomy 21 and CHD
Adriel, BSW
Eleanor Jane, Mosaic Trisomy 18
Jude, Trisomy 18

I dream of these places that
someday I'll go.

My adventurous heart feels
like it may overflow.

Evangeline, Trisomy 18
Beau, Congenital Adrenal Hyperplasia
Grace, Omphalocele, BPD, CHD
Case, PVL Cerebral Palsy
Elijah, Trisomy 21, CHD

Then, one magical day,
my mom strolls on in

With a wagon built for me,
and my travels begin!

Theo, Trisomy 13
Reid, Trisomy 21
and Hirschsprung's Disease
Sebastian, Autism
Gabriel, Trisomy 18
Maria, Trisomy 18

All my medical stuff wheels
right along on our quest.

My tummy feels queezy,
but it's simply the best!!

Emerson, HIE, spastic CP, and Epilepsy
JJ, Severe HIE
Raiden, Autism
Harper, Undiagnosed Genetic Condition
Maddox, Bronchopulmonary Dysplasia

The first place we go,
there are strange things
that move.

They're a little scary,
but I tell my mom I approve.

ZOO
River, CP and Lennox G Syndrome
Matthias, Marfan Syndrome
and Autism
CJ, Trisomy 21 and CP
Ava, Trisomy 18
Declan, 4q deletion 28. 3-31.21

The next place we conquer
is a dark forest road.

But I stand fierce at the
front of my noble abode!

Caleb, Trisomy 21
Kataleya, Trisomy 13
Everest, 22q11.2 Deletion Syndrome
Hutt, TAR Syndrome
Taylor, Trisomy 18

Our next adventure leads
us to a tent on a trail.

Dad says we're camping,
and he's missed no detail.

Jasper, HLHS
Westyn, Spina Bifida, Hydrocephalus
Kayden, Autism
Leo, HIE
Kaiden, Heterotaxy,
Myelodysplastic Syndrome

Another place we venture
has bright lights and
lots of shops.

Mom gets me a stuffie as
we make many stops.

Alejandro, Trisomy 18
Ollie, HIE and Cerebral Palsy
Tynleigh Hope, EOE
Haddie, Trisomy 18
Kenna, Angelman
Syndrome and Epilepsy

I'm traveling the world,
and my dreams feel fulfilled.

I don't think I could be
any more thrilled!

Ember, Autism
Sarah Cate, Trisomy 18 and Spina Bifida
Cayson, Trisomy 21
Miller, Esophageal Atresia
Peter, Trisomy 21

But then, one place we go,
I'm taken out of my wagon perch

My eyes dart around as I try to research.

Tillman, Mosaic T21, CHD
Hudson, Cerebral Palsy
Aspen, Hydrocephalus
King JaKhai, T21 & Cystic Fibrosis
Theo, Trisomy 13

We sit on a seat with people
all around.

And my mom says, "Look, honey, the
wheels are off the ground!"

Ivy, Quad Spastic Cerbral Palsy
Henry and Archie, TOF
Eliott, Cystic Fibrosis
Terry Ann, Trisomy 9

When I wake up from my nap,
We all get up to leave.

My wagon is there when we
walk out the door; I can't believe!

Addison, Preemie
Tucker, Preemie
Blaize, Trisomy 21
Aaliyah, Trisomy 13
Willow, Rett Syndrome

My dad sets me in, and
he says I'm a real traveler now.

But I know my wagon has taken me
farther than many knew how.

Charlie, Trisomy 16
Deskin, Cerebral Palsy
Chayton, Seizures
Anna, Trisomy 13
Mackenzie, CP, 17q12 Microduplication

This was just the beginning
of my many adventures and tales.

There were many more airplanes,
boats, museums, and trails.

Cameron, Trisomy 18
Isaiah, MEND Syndrome
Judah, Spastic Quadriplegia CP
Aislynn, Tango2 Disease
Maria, Trisomy 18
MUSEUM

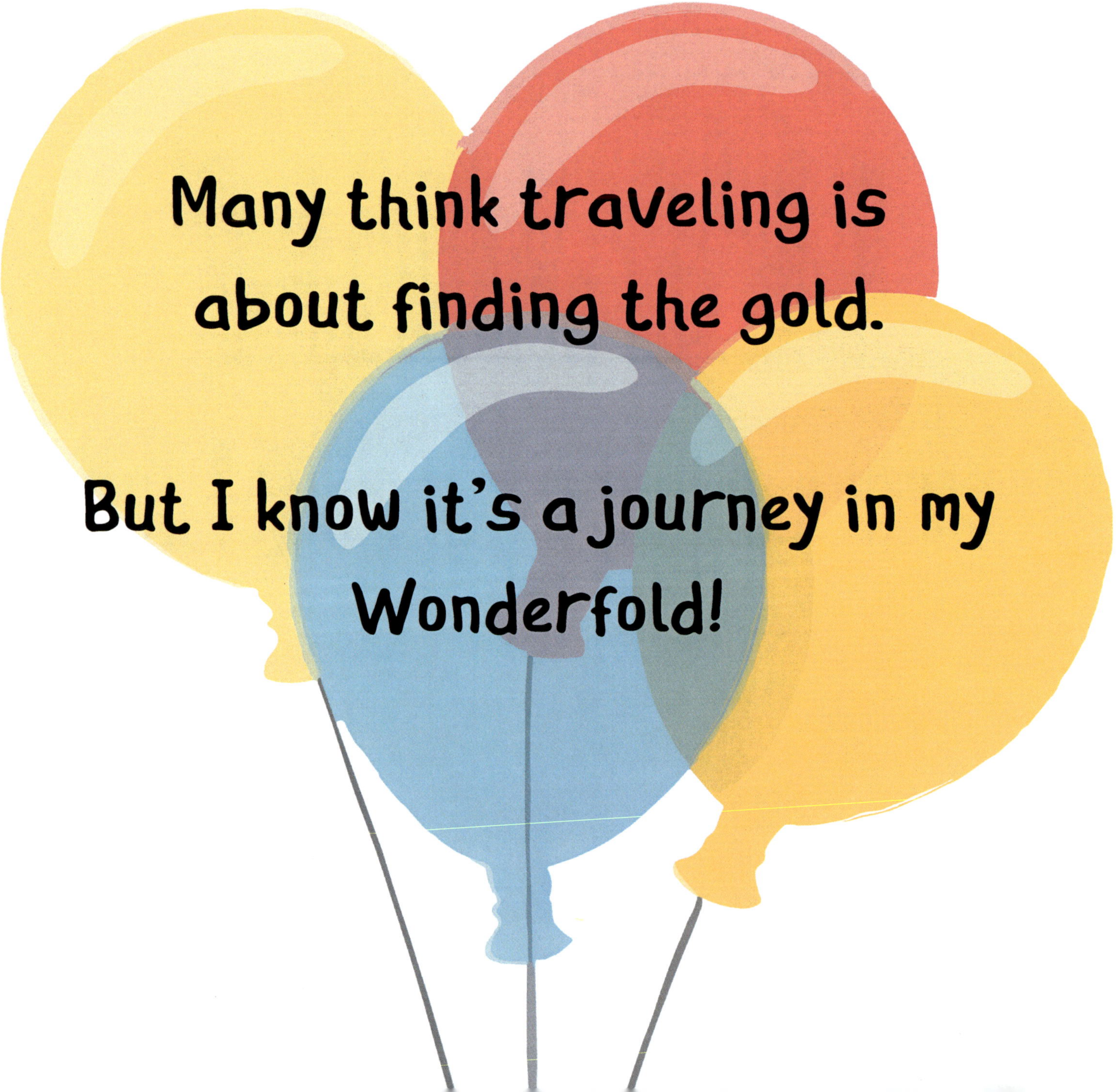

Many think traveling is
about finding the gold.

But I know it's a journey in my
Wonderfold!

Braelynn, CHD
Leo, CHD
Dalton, Chiari 1, tethard cord
Henryk, HLHS
Sam, ASD and Bone Condition
Lydia, Genetic Disorder

Brynleigh Raine, BWS,
Omphalocele
Megean, Trisomy 21
Luna, Primary Caritine
Deficiency
Lilia, Micro Preemie
Caroline, Trisomy 13

Finley, Autism
Beau, CHD, Omphalocele
Dionte, Quadriplegia CP
Kai, Digeorge Syndrome, CHD
Sylvester, Micro Preemie

Travel
ALBUM

Lux, Trisomy 21
Cornelia, Brown's Syndrome
Paxlyn, HIE
Azalea, Septo Optic Dysplasia
Joshua and Declan, Mucolipidosis type 2

Thank You!
WONDERFOLD®
Zechariah
Heart Warrior and Lovingly Adopted, just like Abel!

On August 26, 2023, Abel passed away suddenly.
He stabilized briefly to say goodbye
to his family, friends and primary nurses.

He is greatly loved and missed beyond words.

Abel will continue to live on through his books; inspiring hope, and showing the worth and love of these amazing children no matter the limitation or the duration of their beautiful lives.

Watch for the next books in the Born Abel Book Series:

This is... A Heart Defect   This is... Trisomy 21

The Friendship of the Knitted Hat

Be sure to get your copies of Abel's first 15 books, 1st Workbook, 3 Classes, 10 Coloring/Activity Books, 3 Journals & 2 Books of the Born Mighty Series, 1 This is... Series: All available on Amazon.com

Remember:

All proceeds from the Born Abel Book Series go directly to the Born Abel Foundation!

Abel's Books Are ALL Available on Amazon.com

Born Abel Series

I Am Abel Amazingly Abeled Kids
The Case of the Missing Belly Button
The Mystery of the Patchwork Heart
NICU Neighbors
'Twas the Night Before Discharge
How Angels Are Made
The Big Deal Birthday
The Soft Landing
Leary the Leprechaun
The Colorful Egg Hunt
The Great Baby Wait
What is a Mother?
Where is Heaven?
Super Hero Dad
The Extra Gift
Minds of All Kinds
Oh The Places You'll Stroll

This is... Series

This is... Omphalocele
This is... Trisomy 18

Activity Story Books

The Elf By Himself
My Brother's Birthday in Heaven
My Sister's Birthday in Heaven
The Extraordinarily Different Costume Party

Other Activity Books

Big Top Abel-ities
Trachies, Tubies and Wheelies
Just a Little Bump in the Road - Omphalocele
More Than a Pair - Trisomy 21
Abel's First Workbook

Classes

Nurture and Nature
Nurture and Nature: How Plants Grow
Nurture and Nature: Animal Habitats
Nurture and Nature: Seasonal Changes
Nurture and Nature: HoneyBees

Journals

Bee Mine Valentine
Navigating the NICU
NICU Journal: Brave Little Mustard Seed

Born Mighty Series

Babies Born Brave
Who's Who in the NICU?

Remember: All Proceeds Go To the BORN ABEL FOUNDATION

Published in the United States of America

Authentic Endeavors Publishing / Book Endeavors
Clarks Summit PA 18411

Born Abel: Oh, The Places You'll Stroll

Paperback ISBN: 978-1-963849-45-5

Born Abel Book Series

Made in United States
North Haven, CT
09 September 2024